The 7 Bricks:

Building Foundations for Leadership, Growth, and Lasting Impact

By

Dr. Joshua Bowles

ISBN: 979-8-234-04261-3

Published by Seven Bricks Press

First Edition

Cover design by Dr. Joshua Bowles

Printed in the United States of America

To my beautiful wife, who has stood beside me through every step of this journey—and continues to help build the foundation we stand on.

Table of Contents

Preface

Full disclosure: while my career has been rooted in education, I am not a traditional educator. In truth, very little about my background or professional path would be considered conventional. I hold a doctorate degree specializing in executive leadership and have spent years studying teaching methodologies, leadership theory, and organizational strategy. My work has focused on both educational and healthcare leadership, continuing education, and professional development, and I have developed a strong foundation in both instructional practice and leadership frameworks. However, those credentials are not the reason this book exists. My education has introduced me to people, experiences, and opportunities that have shaped my perspective and expanded my world. But there are many individuals far more deeply rooted in academic theory who have written exceptional books on leadership models and step-by-step frameworks. I respect that work. I have learned from it. If that is what you are seeking, there are outstanding resources available to you. This is not one of those books. This is not a formula in the traditional sense. It is not a universal field guide. It does not attempt to offer a one-size-fits-all solution. Instead, this book approaches leadership from a different angle—one shaped by experience, observation, and the realities of environments where people either break or build.

In addition to my work in education, I am an athletic trainer—an allied health professional trained to evaluate, treat, and rehabilitate athletic related injuries. Interestingly, it was this path that ultimately led me into education. Operating in both spaces has provided a unique lens through which I have come to understand leadership: in moments of pressure, in environments that demand trust, decisions carry immediate and lasting consequences. Many of those experiences are woven through this book.

I am also a follower of Jesus Christ. While this book is not written as a theological work, my faith is foundational to how I lead. As a result, there are moments where biblical principles and references are included—not as prescriptions, but as part of the story that has shaped my perspective. I believe each person is equipped with the ability to think, discern, and choose their own path. My intention is not to impose belief, but to be transparent about the foundation from which I operate.

How we learn is often just as important as what we learn—and sometimes even more important than why we learn. Growth rarely comes from perfectly structured systems alone; it is often forged through experience, challenge, and reflection.

My hope is that what you find in these pages resonates in an unconventional way—that it challenges your thinking, sharpens your awareness, and sparks ideas of your own.

Because in the end, this is not just about leadership.

It's about what you choose to build with what you have been given.

Introduction

There are walls in every life. Some are obvious. Others are invisible. Some were built to protect us. Others were built because we didn't know what else to do. Over time, those walls become part of who we are. They shape how we think, how we respond, and how we interact with the people around us. At first, they serve a purpose. They keep us safe from failure. They protect us from embarrassment. They give us a sense of control when things feel uncertain. But eventually, something begins to change. The same walls that once protected us start to limit us. They keep us from growing, and they keep us from connecting. They keep us from becoming who we're capable of becoming. And most of the time, we don't even realize they are there.

I've seen this play out repeatedly—not just in my own life, but in the lives of athletes, students, and individuals I've worked with throughout my career. In athletic training, people rarely break down all at once. It doesn't usually come from one major injury. It comes from small things.

A slight imbalance.

A missed movement pattern.

A compensation that seems harmless at first.

Over time, those small things add up. The body adapts in ways it shouldn't. Other areas begin to take on more stress. Eventually, what started as something minor becomes something that can't be ignored.

The system breaks down. And when that happens, there are two options:

Cover it up or rebuild it.

The same is true in leadership. The same is true in education. The same is true in life.

We all build walls—brick by brick—through experiences, failures, fears, and habits. Those walls feel strong. They feel safe. But they are often built on weak foundations. And when pressure comes, those walls don't hold.

They crack.

They collapse.

And we're left trying to figure out what to do next. Most people focus on tearing the walls down. But very few focus on what to build in their place. That's where this book begins.

Because breaking down walls is not enough.

If we don't replace them with something stronger, we will rebuild the same walls all over again. This book introduces a different way of thinking. Instead of using bricks to build walls, what if we used them to build a foundation?

A foundation that supports growth instead of limiting it.

A foundation that connects people instead of separating them.

A foundation that allows individuals, teams, and classrooms to thrive.

It's for individuals who know they're capable of more but feel stuck behind something they can't quite name. You don't need to tear everything down overnight. You don't need to have all the answers right now. You just need to start placing the right bricks. Because walls are built the same way they're broken. Brick by brick. And if you're willing to build something stronger in their place—you may find that the walls you once depended on were never what you needed at all.

Chapter 1

Brick and Mortar

"Your own words are the bricks and mortar of the dreams you want to realize."

Sonia Choquette

Brick and Mortar

Have you ever thought about how brick walls are made? Hardened clay that is crafted to form bricks is layered together with mortar, a close relative of concrete, to create a solid, foundational structure that is either meant to serve as one piece of a support structure or to be used to keep something in or even to keep something from getting out. The phrase “brick and mortar” is synonymous with storefronts or restaurants that have their own structure in place. Food trucks that turn into “brick and mortar” are transitioning from a mobile, flexible structure to a permanent, fixed structure. When we think of a brick-and-mortar wall, we tend to think of that wall as being a good, firm piece of a larger solid foundation. As *The Three Little Pigs* taught us, a house made of brick was indeed stronger than a house made of sticks or straw. While this method of building walls may not be the most absolute in terms of permanence, most of us tend to think of this style when we think of a strong wall being built. It's easy to see why. They represent something solid and firm.

What would you point to in your life that represents something solid and firm? Perhaps your faith? Family? Health? Career? In reality, some of these may not last forever. At a certain time in our lives, change is inevitable. However, oftentimes we look to how we can secure the things around us we hold dear to create a solid and firm foundation. In essence, we build walls. These walls might be providing security and support for our families or providing a loving home, perhaps even landing that job you have been hoping for. How about something earlier in our lives? Take graduating from high school, for example. This is an accomplishment in a young adult's life that represents the transition from childhood to adulthood. The transition from one step of education to another step of education. Maybe another step of fiscal responsibility in the form of entering the workforce. As each of these events in life takes place, we are metaphorically throwing down a thin layer of mortar and placing one brick firmly in place, lining it up with the ones below it and beside it. We are adding to our solid foundation. We are creating security, prosperity, and comfort. We are building walls.

Everyone builds walls. Brick by brick, the experiences we have in life create another moment that may involve us placing another brick in our wall. Sometimes in life, these are negative experiences. A loss of a job, or the death of a close loved one, or even a breakup that created pain and suffering could produce an unwanted brick. We place bricks on our walls for these experiences as well. These tend to look and feel a bit different, however. When too many of these bricks go up, the wall becomes a different form of security. We are now building a defensive wall.

With some events in our lives, one or two bricks may be placed. However, maybe you've heard someone say that they have "thrown up a wall" due to a major negative event that occurred in their life. These are likely not just one or two bricks over time, but rather a few dump trucks full of bricks all at once. These walls can create defensiveness, embarrassment, limited self-worth, or even shame.

Often these characteristics are hidden behind the walls we have built to allow us to remain functional and go about our lives. Our hope is these walls protect us from whatever happened in the past so that we may not be negatively affected or hurt by similar events. Unfortunately, this is not the case. If this were true, we would never experience any pain or suffering after the first encounter again. I have experienced a loss from a relationship ending. Did I put up a wall for that event? Of course, I did. I placed this defense mechanism to guard against the feeling of pain or loss again. Did additional moments of pain or loss occur again? You bet! These walls are not impenetrable forces never to be tested again. We repeat this cycle many times in our lives, some of us to the point that we become hardened and disassociated with the more beautiful aspects of our lives.

The old phrase "stop and smell the roses" was always humorous to me. Rarely in my day do I come across roses for me to just stop and smell. When I do see roses, I typically don't adjust my day to go smell them. But of course, this quote was not meant to be taken so literally. The roses are meant to be anything in your life that might be beautiful for you to pause and enjoy. Have you ever run into someone in your morning hustle and bustle who asked you, "Did you see the sunrise this morning? Wow, it was beautiful," only to realize that it's been weeks, or months, or perhaps even longer that you've intentionally watched a sunrise? What beauty have you been missing that is all around you every day? My guess is a lot more than you realize.

What is currently happening in your life that you are missing because you are too busy building walls? What if, instead of building up walls, we broke them down? Likely, not every brick we place is done with intention. Some are placed out of fear, some out of habit. But over time, what we build begins to reflect what we believe about ourselves and what we believe about our purpose.

Have you ever met someone you instantly knew had a wall up? Maybe the wall was towards a situation in their life or someone in their life. Maybe the wall was even placed against you. Whatever the reason, how did you perceive this person? Most likely, there was defensiveness and a guarded demeanor towards the situation or the individual. By building up walls, we create a false sense of security. Sure, walls are great for fortifying structures, but are they the best course of action for an individual? Each of us has a brick in one hand and mortar in the other. While these can be used to build a foundation of strength and security, too often we use them to defend ourselves from being hurt or embarrassed or maybe even feeling shame because of a failure.

Schools are one of the best examples of how building up walls can cause destruction. Both students and educators alike can build walls and create defense mechanisms. You may recall a certain teacher who always seemed to be in a bad mood. Or if you were lucky enough, you may have experienced a teacher who always seemed accepting of everyone who walked into their classroom. In which situation do you feel the best learning occurred? Those in the classroom with the closed-off teacher may have missed out on an experience that could enrich their learning environment. We will never know what could have been different if that teacher had decided to break down walls and build a foundation for something better. So many of us today need to know it's acceptable to start breaking down walls. Brick by brick, one piece at a time.

Chapter 2

Jericho

"Men build too many walls and not enough bridges."

Joseph Fort Newton

Jericho

There's a story in the Bible about a man who was called into leadership for an entire civilization of people. His predecessor, Moses, who had led his people out of Egypt, was widely regarded as one of the greatest leaders of all time. The transition from Moses to Joshua provides a powerful example of what it means to step into a role where expectations have been established at the highest level.

Have you ever been tasked with taking over a position from someone who was considered exceptional in that role? This is a common challenge in professional environments. Whether stepping into a leadership position, inheriting a high-performing team, or following a predecessor who set a strong standard, the pressure to "measure up" can be significant.

However, the objective is not to replicate the individual who came before you. The expectation is not to fill their shoes. Those were never yours to begin with. High-performing predecessors do not create a ceiling—they create a reference point. Their success does not define your limitations; it highlights the opportunity in front of you.

Effective professionals understand that stepping into a role is not about replacement—it is about evolution. Every leadership transition, every new role, and every professional opportunity presents a chance to establish a new identity, refine direction, and elevate performance in a way that aligns with your own strengths and vision.

The standard has already been set. Your responsibility is not to mirror it, but to build upon it.

In chapter 1 of the Book of Joshua in the Bible, God passed the torch from Moses to Joshua. God instructed Joshua that he was now to be the leader of His people and that God would uphold His promises to lead all of God's people to the Promised Land. The city of Jericho was a gate city. Anyone who wanted passage from the other side of the Jordan River had to seek travel through the heavily fortified city of Jericho. Jericho, now known as Tell es-Sultan, meaning "Hill of the Sultan", was discovered and confirmed as the biblical historical site by Charles Warren, a member of the British Royal Engineers. Tell es-Sultan is in the modern-day West Bank of Israel on the banks of the Jordan River. The Holy City of Jerusalem is also considered to be a part of the West Bank by international law. What is uniquely fascinating about the story of Jericho is not only was this an impressive city with massive, fortified defensive walls that surrounded the entire city, but by most estimates, it is presumably the oldest city with such walls. Although defensive barriers are a common occurrence now and seldom do we think about the rarity they once were, the city walls of Jericho would have been a structure not commonly seen by most people at that time, and I imagine quite intimidating.

Freestanding structures were a common occurrence in terms of straw, sticks and clay to form a hardened mortar, but the idea of a city with defensive walls was not widely utilized. The oldest walls in existence were from the temple of Gobekli Tepe in what is now, southeastern Turkey. The oldest known city walls are those of Jericho, dating around the 10th century B.C., and the Sumerian city of Uruk. You will find evidence of both sites claiming to be the oldest city with defensive walls, although evidence points to Jericho taking the slight edge.

While the story and lore behind the city of Jericho have been shared and passed on, the foundation behind the impressive victory of Joshua and the Israelites is that the walls of Jericho were meant to awe and intimidate. Walls of this nature had never been seen before and were designed to create a sense of security for those citizens of Jericho. As the leader of the Israelites, Joshua had to rely on his faith and trust in God to succeed. The walls had to come down. If God's people were to make it to the Promised Land, the walls around Jericho had to crumble. It was the tearing down of the walls that provided opportunities. The walls didn't fall because of strength alone. They fell because of the obedience and faith Joshua placed in something greater than the obstacle itself.

Much like the metaphorical walls we build in our own lives, the walls of Jericho served multiple purposes. The walls were used as protection and shelter against any potential threat. The same is true of the walls we build up in our lives. Often when something negative happens, we turn back behind the wall to shield us. The failures that we experience can lead us to build more walls, brick by brick.

Like the story of Jericho though, Joshua had to tear down the walls to fulfill the promise that God had made to his people.

The only way to move past any failures or obstacles we encounter in our lives is to move past the walls.

We build up these walls in our lives and our careers, to be a defensive barrier and a form of protection and security. We want to keep what is inside safe and we don't want anything from the outside to jeopardize that. From one perspective, that's essential! Of course, teachers want to keep students safe; employers want to keep their employees safe; and we want to protect and hold onto our ideals, our methods, and our structure. But let's evaluate this from another perspective. If we are constantly keeping out other ideas and potential growth opportunities, we will never reach the possibilities that could exist.

Many professions have some form of continuing education, sometimes known as professional development. What does this really mean? Any form of continuing education is designed to further enhance the knowledge and skills beyond what was gained from formal education. In other words, your learning and growth shouldn't stop just because you graduated, earned your degree, and perhaps obtained additional training or a certification. What if you were about to go in for surgery and learned that the physician about to operate on you has been practicing medicine for 20 years, but hasn't bothered to stay up to date on the latest research or enhance his or her skills since graduating from medical school? Would you be completely comfortable with that? The same is true for educators and administrators alike. The same is also true for those in corporate America.

Your knowledge and skill set should be constantly improving. This involves breaking down walls.

There are a few key principles that I will address in this book that I find to be essential in breaking down walls. I call them the 7 Bricks.

These bricks are used differently. Instead of building up walls, we will use these bricks to lay a foundation on which all walls can be broken down. Many years ago, the time came for the walls of Jericho to fall. It's time for our own walls to fall.

Chapter 3

Failure

"I've failed over and over again in my life and that is why I succeed."

Michael Jordan

Failure

Before we go any further, I feel obligated to share with you that I have failed, many times. I'm not ashamed of that.

Failure is not something to avoid or hide from. It's something to understand. In this life, failure is not optional, it's inevitable. The difference is how we respond to it.

Any success I may have achieved has not come without setbacks. I have earned a doctorate, but that did not come from a straight path. That achievement came through struggle, adjustment, and failure. High school came easily for me. College did not. By the time I arrived, the experience hit me like a brick wall. I struggled through my first three semesters, so much so that I was placed on academic probation, and eventually academic suspension. The university made it clear that I was not meeting the required academic standards, and without immediate improvement, I would be placed on academic suspension. I didn't improve. I failed—in more ways than one.

After I was placed on academic suspension, I moved to the Nashville, Tennessee area. I worked a few odd jobs for my father to make a little bit of money. One of those jobs involved driving a van delivering dog food to customers' homes. It didn't take long to realize that if I didn't change direction, that path could become permanent. That moment forced a decision. I needed to rethink what I wanted from my college experience and commit to working toward a clear goal.

Failure is going to happen. A setback is a failure that needs to be examined. There's a common phrase: "*For every door that closes, another opens*." In reality, that's not how it usually works. For most of us, whenever one door closes, several more close with it. What we need to understand is that for every failure, for every no, or for every time we are told not right now, there is an eventual opportunity down the road. It may not look the way we expect. It may not come when we want it to. But it exists.

Some assume that phrase comes from the Bible. It doesn't. Jesus never promised that for every door that closes, another will automatically open. Alexander Graham Bell famously quoted, *"When one door closes, another opens."* The opportunity is there—but it does not remove responsibility. Failure does not close the door. Inaction does. Complacency does.

We will all experience failure. That is not optional. Failure is part of the process—part of growth, part of progress, part of becoming capable of handling what comes next. The difference is not in who fails, but in who responds. Goals are not meant to be easy. If something can be achieved quickly and without resistance, it likely lacks the depth required for meaningful growth. Real progress demands challenge. It requires effort, discipline, and persistence through setbacks.

Failure is not a detour—it is part of the path.

Failure has a way of challenging what we believe about ourselves. It can also clarify it, if we are willing to keep moving forward instead of letting it define us.

Each setback carries information. Each mistake creates awareness. Each failure, when handled correctly, becomes a step forward rather than a step back. Over time, those steps compound into something greater than any immediate success ever could.

Many people define credibility by their accomplishments—their degrees, their titles, and their success. And to be clear, those are meaningful indicators. They represent effort, discipline, and achievement. But they are not the full picture. There is another form of credibility that is often overlooked—the kind built through failure. The setbacks endured and the work required to recover. The persistence to continue when progress is not guaranteed. That type of credibility cannot be manufactured. Success without struggle lacks depth. It lacks the perspective that only failure can provide.

To achieve something great, it helps to understand what it means to be knocked down and choose to continue anyway. You must experience resistance, adjust, and move forward with greater awareness. Those moments: the setbacks, the missteps, the challenges, are not just obstacles. These are what give success its weight. They are what make it credible.

Learning, in many ways takes the same form. For all of us, learning requires some setbacks. Experience helps create those ingrained moments and skills that, when developed, can lead to achievements. Think about a recent skill you tried to learn. Chances are, there may have been a setback or two. What if you played a sport? How about the first time you tried to make a basket from the 3-point arc, or tried to catch a football, or perhaps the first time you swung a golf club; how did that go? Maybe it didn't go well. These setbacks create a desire to work hard, create repetition, and improve.

Failures in life create pathways to achievements and opportunity. Learning takes place the same way. Progress is rarely linear. Setbacks are part of how growth happens.

Do not fear failure. Be terrified of regret.

At the beginning of this chapter, I shared several examples of failure in my own life. Like Jericho, those walls had to come down. Not to leave a void, but to make room for something stronger. Something that could support growth, could sustain progress, and ultimately lead to success.

Chapter 4

The 7 Bricks

"We've got to rebuild human hearts – and persuade people that hope isn't just possible, but essential."

Tony Snow

The 7 Bricks

Early in my athletic training career, I worked with an athlete who came in with what seemed like a minor issue—just some tightness in the hamstring. No major injury. No defining moment. Just something that had been lingering long enough to become noticeable. At first, it didn't look like much, but as we evaluated further, the real issue started to reveal itself. What began as a small imbalance had quietly spread. The athlete had started compensating without realizing it. Movement patterns had shifted. The hip wasn't firing correctly. The lower back was starting to take on more load. Even the opposite leg was beginning to show signs of weakness. Nothing had "failed" in the traditional sense.

But everything was starting to break down.

And that's what stuck with me.

The body doesn't always need a major event to fall apart. It can happen gradually. Quietly. One small compensation at a time—until eventually, the system can't sustain itself anymore.

Breaking something down is easy. Rebuilding it is not.

Rehabilitation didn't happen in one session. There wasn't a quick fix. We had to slow everything down. We had to retrain movement. We had to rebuild strength in areas that had been neglected. We had to focus on the fundamentals—one step at a time, one movement at a time. It was a process. And it required intention. That experience changed how I saw more than just injuries. It changed how I saw people, growth, and leadership. Because just like the body, we don't suddenly fall apart overnight. Breakdown happens gradually.

Brick by brick.

If we're not intentional about what we build back in its place, we'll find ourselves repeating the same patterns. Breaking something down is often easier than building. Walls can come down quickly. Sometimes all it takes is one moment, one realization, or one failure to begin tearing down the barriers we've built in our lives.

In the previous chapters, we explored how those walls are formed brick by brick through experience, failure, fear, and even success. We also explored the necessity of breaking those walls down. But breaking down walls is only the beginning. Because once the walls fall, something else must take their place.

If nothing replaces those walls, we risk rebuilding the same structures all over again. The same fears, the same defensive habits, the same patterns of isolation will slowly creep back in.

So, the question becomes:

If we are not building walls…what are we building?

The answer is a foundation.

Walls are designed to separate, to protect, and sometimes to isolate. Foundations, however, are designed to support. They hold things together rather than keep things apart. They create stability without creating division. Foundations are not built all at once. They are built one piece at a time. Brick by brick.

For most of our lives, we have used bricks to build walls. Every experience—good or bad—has added another layer. Over time, those bricks have created structures that feel safe but often limit growth, connection, and opportunity.

What if those same bricks could be used differently? What if instead of building walls, we used them to build something that supports growth rather than restricts it? That is where the concept of the 7 Bricks comes into play. These bricks are not meant to build barriers. They are meant to build a foundation strong enough that walls are no longer needed.

The 7 Bricks are principles—core elements of leadership and growth that, when placed intentionally, create an environment where individuals and organizations can thrive.

The 7 Bricks are:

- Leadership
- Integrity
- Unity
- Communication
- Confidence
- Servanthood
- Environment

Each brick serves a purpose:

Leadership provides direction.

Integrity builds trust.

Unity creates strength.

Communication brings clarity.

Confidence fuels growth.

Servanthood centers purpose.

Environment sustains everything.

Individually, each of these bricks carries its own weight. Together, they form something powerful—a foundation.

These principles are not just strategies, they are commitments. Over time, what we consistently commit to begins to shape not only what we build, but who we become.

One of the main differences between a wall and a foundation is a foundation is often unseen. It doesn't draw attention to itself. Yet everything built on top of it depends on its strength.

In education, in business, and in life, this distinction matters greatly. Too often, systems are built like walls—rigid structures designed to control outcomes, protect processes, and maintain order. While structure is important, when it becomes too rigid, it can limit creativity, discourage growth, and isolate individuals within the system.

Students begin to feel confined rather than supported.

Educators begin to feel restricted rather than empowered.

Employees begin to feel invisible rather than valued.

Walls may create order, but they rarely create growth. Foundations, however, create opportunity. When a strong foundation is in place, individuals are free to grow, to explore, and to build something meaningful on top of it. In a classroom built on a strong foundation, students feel safe to take risks. They feel supported in their learning. They understand that failure is part of the process, not something to be avoided at all costs.

In leadership, the same principle applies. Leaders who build walls often rely on control, authority, and rigid structures. Leaders who build foundations focus on people, trust, and growth.

One approach limits. The other expands.

The imagery of building "one brick at a time" is important because growth does not happen all at once.

No leader becomes effective overnight. No student masters a concept instantly. No organization transforms in a single moment. Progress is built gradually. One decision at a time. One interaction at a time. One brick at a time. Earlier, we recognized that many of the bricks we place are unintentional, often forming the very walls that limit us. That must change. These 7 Bricks must now be placed with purpose.

If a brick is missing, the foundation weakens. If a brick is placed carelessly, instability follows. But when each brick is placed with purpose, something strong begins to form. This is not about perfection. It is about progress. You will not always place every brick perfectly. There will be moments where leadership falters, where communication breaks down, or where confidence wavers. That is part of the process. Remember that failure can be used for good. The goal is not to avoid mistakes, but to continue building despite them.

Most people spend their lives pouring energy into the wrong structure—without realizing they could be using the same bricks to build something impactful.

As we move forward, each of the next chapters will focus on one of these bricks. We will explore what each one means, why it matters, and how it contributes to the overall foundation.

Because breaking down walls is not enough.

We must replace them with something stronger.

That strength is built—one brick at a time.

Chapter 5

Leadership: The First Brick

"A leader is one who knows the way, goes the way, and shows the way."

John C. Maxwell

Leadership

John C. Maxwell is known as one of the most influential leadership experts in the world. Having authored over 100 books on the subject, he is well known for the principle that "leadership is influence – nothing more, nothing less."

Early in his career, Maxwell took over a struggling church where attendance was low and morale was even lower. The congregation was discouraged and frustrated, there was no sense of direction for the church. Maxwell decided that instead of trying to overhaul everything or assert his authority as the new leader of the church, he would turn his focus to the people. He met with individuals one on one to listen to their concerns, learning their stories and took time to invest in their growth. Slowly, things started to change. People began to feel valued. Leaders began to emerge from within the group. Over time, the organization didn't just improve, it was transformed. Maxwell's impact wasn't confined to a single church or even the multiple churches that he helped develop and lead - it expanded into millions of leaders worldwide. Great leadership doesn't just fix a place—it multiplies influence far beyond it.

Leadership is often misunderstood. Many people assume leadership is about authority, position, or status. Titles may indicate responsibility, but they do not create leadership. Leadership begins the moment someone decides to take responsibility for the direction of others. In many organizations, schools, and teams, people wait for leadership to come from above. They assume someone else will provide direction, someone else will solve problems, and someone else will take the first step forward.

When everyone waits, nothing moves.

Leadership is the first brick in the foundation because someone must go first. Without leadership, organizations drift. Corporations begin to lose. Classrooms lose focus. Teams fracture. Individuals become uncertain about their purpose and direction. Leadership provides the clarity that allows others to move forward with confidence. In education, leadership is particularly important because educators do far more than deliver information. Teachers shape environments. They influence culture. They help students understand not only what they are learning, but why learning matters. Students instinctively recognize leadership. They know when a teacher is confident in their direction and when uncertainty dominates the room. Leadership creates a sense of stability and expectation. Students thrive when expectations are clear and when someone is guiding them forward.

Leadership also requires courage. When challenges arise—and they inevitably will—the leader cannot retreat behind walls of avoidance or blame. Leadership requires stepping forward in moments of uncertainty.

In many ways, leadership is less about control and more about responsibility. The best leaders are not those who dictate every action of those around them, but those who create a vision others are willing to follow.

The first brick in breaking down walls involves leadership. Leaders by their very nature help create change and movement. Someone must be willing to move forward even when others hesitate. Leadership begins when someone decides that waiting is no longer an option. Stepping forward often requires trusting a direction that isn't fully visible. For me, that requires faith—not that the path will be easy, but that it will become clear through movement. Leadership is not revealed in moments of comfort, but in moments of uncertainty. When everything is going well, leadership can appear effortless. The real test comes when the path forward is unclear, when obstacles begin to rise, and others start to question whether progress is still possible.

In those moments, people look for direction. Students look to teachers. Teams look to coaches. Organizations look to leaders. Someone must decide that standing still is no longer acceptable and that moving forward—even cautiously—is better than remaining trapped behind walls.

Leadership begins when someone accepts that responsibility. The most effective leaders rarely see themselves as the most important person in the room. Instead, they see themselves as the person responsible for ensuring that everyone else can succeed. Leadership becomes less about personal recognition and more about creating momentum for others.

When leadership is grounded in responsibility rather than ego, it becomes powerful. However, leadership alone is not enough to sustain a foundation. A leader may provide direction,

but direction without trust quickly collapses. Followers may move forward for a time, but if they question the character of the person guiding them, uncertainty will soon take hold.
Leadership may place the first brick in the foundation, but the strength of that brick depends on something deeper.

The next brick that must be placed is integrity.

Because leadership without integrity cannot hold.

Chapter 6

Integrity: The Second Brick

"Integrity is doing the right thing, even when no one is watching."

C.S. Lewis

Integrity

C.S. Lewis has always been a fascinating individual to study. Before C.S. Lewis became one of the most influential Christian writers of the 20th century, he was a committed atheist. As a professor at Oxford, Lewis valued logic, reason, and intellectual honesty above all else. But over time, through conversations with close friends like J.R.R. Tolkien, author of *The Lord of the Rings* saga, and through his own reading and reflection, he began to feel that his beliefs didn't fully align with the evidence he was encountering.

What makes Lewis remarkable is what he did next.

He didn't ignore it. He didn't protect his pride or cling to his previous position for the sake of reputation. Instead, he followed the truth as he understood it—even though it meant completely changing his worldview. Lewis eventually became a Christian, not because it was comfortable or popular in his circles, but because he believed it was true. He demonstrated integrity to his readers because he was true to himself.

Leadership without integrity collapses quickly. A leader may hold authority for a time, but without trust, that authority eventually dissolves. People follow leaders they trust, not leaders they simply fear or obey. Integrity is consistency between what we say and what we do. Students notice integrity immediately. In fact, young people are often better judges of authenticity than adults. They can sense when someone is genuine and when someone is merely performing a role. A teacher who speaks about discipline but behaves inconsistently erodes credibility quickly. Integrity builds trust, and trust builds stability. In education and leadership alike, trust allows individuals to take risks. Students must feel safe enough to fail, to ask questions, and to challenge their own understanding.

When integrity is present, students believe that their educators have their best interests in mind.

Without integrity, walls begin to rise. People become defensive. Communication becomes guarded. Innovation slows. Individuals begin protecting themselves rather than contributing to a shared mission. Integrity is not about perfection. Every leader will make mistakes. Every educator will experience moments where decisions could have been handled better. Integrity does not demand flawlessness; it demands accountability.

Admitting mistakes does not weaken credibility—it strengthens it. When students see adults take responsibility for their actions, they learn that character matters more than appearance. They learn that honesty is stronger than image. Integrity is the second brick because no foundation can stand without trust.

Trust turns leadership into influence.

Integrity is revealed over time. Anyone can speak convincingly for a moment. Anyone can present themselves well in the right circumstances. Integrity, however, is measured by the consistency of our actions across many moments—especially when those moments are difficult.

Students observe this carefully. Employees notice changes. They notice when expectations change depending on convenience. They recognize when fairness is applied inconsistently.

The same is true in healthcare. Patients may not understand every diagnosis or treatment plan, but they understand consistency. They recognize when a provider is honest and when care is delivered with intention. They also recognize when something feels rushed, inconsistent, or uncertain. They can see when words and actions begin to drift apart.

Integrity eliminates that drift. When individuals know what to expect from a leader, stability forms. Stability allows people to focus their energy on growth rather than self-protection.

Trust becomes the result. Trust allows teams to take risks together. Trust allows classrooms to become places of curiosity rather than fear. Trust allows individuals to work together without constantly questioning motives.

Integrity creates the conditions where collaboration becomes possible. Yet integrity, by itself, does not automatically create connection between people. Even when individuals trust one another, they must still learn how to work together toward shared goals.

Integrity builds trust. But trust must be directed somewhere.

That direction leads us to the third brick—unity.

Because once trust exists, people must learn to move forward together.

Chapter 7

Unity: The Third Brick

"Alone we can do little; together we can do so much."

Helen Keller

Unity

As a young child, Helen Keller lost both her sight and her hearing due to illness, leaving her isolated in a world she could neither see nor hear. Frustrated and unable to communicate, she often lashed out because she had no way to connect with others. Her world was completely separated from everyone around her—a life behind invisible walls. Everything began to change when her teacher, Anne Sullivan, entered her life. Anne didn't just try to teach Helen—she joined her world. She patiently spelled words into Helen's hand, over and over again, forming a connection where none had existed. For a long time, it seemed like nothing was working. Then one day, as water flowed over Helen's hand, Anne spelled out the word "water." Suddenly, something clicked. Helen realized that everything had a name—and more importantly, that she could connect with others. From that moment forward, Helen was no longer alone.

Human beings are wired for community. Teams succeed because individuals combine their abilities, perspectives, and strengths. Unity transforms individual effort into collective strength. In education, unity means recognizing that learning is not a solitary experience. Classrooms function best when students feel connected to one another and to the mission of the class itself.

Competition can motivate individuals, but collaboration builds sustainable growth. Unity does not mean uniformity. Individuals bring different talents, personalities, and perspectives to the table. The strength of unity lies precisely in these differences. When diverse abilities are directed toward a shared goal, the result is far greater than any individual effort.

Teams in athletics illustrate this clearly. A championship team is rarely composed solely of the most talented individual players. Instead, successful teams are built around shared purpose and trust among teammates.

The same principle applies to classrooms and organizations. When unity exists, individuals stop asking, "What do I gain?" and begin asking, "What can we accomplish together?" Walls thrive on division. When individuals feel isolated, misunderstood, or excluded, defensive barriers appear quickly. Unity breaks those barriers by reminding individuals that they belong to something larger than themselves. Students learn better when they feel connected. Educators work more effectively when collaboration replaces competition.

Unity is the third brick because foundations grow stronger when individuals work together.

Walls separate.

Unity connects.

Unity requires more than alignment; it requires humility. Unity requires a willingness to value something greater than individual recognition.

When individuals feel connected to a shared purpose, something remarkable begins to happen. People start encouraging one another rather than competing with one another. Success becomes something that is celebrated collectively rather than guarded individually. Teams begin to form. This is why environments built on unity often outperform those built solely on individual achievement. When people believe they are part of something larger than themselves, they invest more deeply in the outcome. Students who feel connected to their classroom participate more willingly. Athletes who feel connected to their teammates push themselves further. Educators who feel connected to their colleagues collaborate more freely.

Unity removes isolation.

However, unity cannot survive without something that continually reinforces it. Even strong teams can fracture when misunderstandings grow or when assumptions replace clarity. Without clear communication, unity slowly erodes. Silence allows confusion to grow. Confusion creates frustration. Frustration eventually rebuilds the very walls that unity worked so hard to dismantle. Unity must therefore be protected through something stronger than intention. It must be reinforced through communication.

Because the strength of any team depends on how well its members understand one another.

Chapter 8

Communication: The Fourth Brick

"The single biggest problem in communication is the illusion that it has taken place."

George Bernard Shaw

Communication

A professor in London named Henry Higgins believes that language and speech is everything. The year is 1912, and Professor Higgins sets out to prove this theory by attempting to transform a poor flower girl into a refined lady. The professor believes that by simply teaching the uneducated lower-class girl correct pronunciation and polished language, she can pass as someone from high society. In many ways, he succeeds—the young girl learns the words, the sounds, and the structure of communication.

But something unexpected happens.

Even after mastering speech, the young girl begins to feel misunderstood, frustrated, and disconnected. Higgins had taught her how to speak, but he never truly learned how to listen or understand her as a person. Their conflict reveals a deeper truth: communication is not just about words—it's about connection, empathy, and understanding.

The young girl's name was Eliza Doolittle. The story was written by George Bernard Shaw in a play titled *Pygmalion,* which was later adapted to become the story and eventually the classic movie, *My Fair Lady*, starring Audrey Hepburn and Rex Harrison.

Miscommunication builds walls faster than almost any other force.

When individuals stop communicating clearly, assumptions replace understanding. When assumptions dominate, misunderstandings multiply. Walls begin to rise between individuals who might otherwise have worked together.

Communication is more than speaking. It involves listening, understanding, and responding with clarity and respect. In educational environments, communication is foundational. Students must understand expectations. Teachers must understand student needs. Administrators must communicate vision and support.

Clear communication removes uncertainty.

When individuals know what is expected of them, they perform with greater confidence and focus. When expectations remain unclear, frustration grows and effort declines. Listening is the often-overlooked component of communication. Leaders who listen create environments where people feel valued. Students who feel heard become more engaged in the learning process. When people believe their voices matter, they become more invested in the outcome.

When expectations are clearly defined, healthcare professionals operate with greater confidence, precision, and focus in delivering care. When direction is inconsistent or unclear, uncertainty increases, communication breaks down, and performance can suffer. Equally important is the role of listening, which remains one of the most underutilized skills in healthcare. Providers who listen intentionally create an environment where patients feel involved in their care. When individuals believe their voice matters, high quality outcomes follow.

Communication also requires humility. No individual possesses complete knowledge or understanding. The willingness to listen and learn from others strengthens the entire community.

Walls form when people stop listening.

Communication is the fourth brick because understanding creates connection. Where communication thrives, walls struggle to survive. Communication is the lifeline of every strong organization, classroom, and team. When communication is clear and consistent, problems are addressed quickly and misunderstandings are resolved before they grow into barriers. People feel heard. Expectations remain visible. Progress continues moving forward.

But when communication breaks down, walls begin to rise again. Individuals begin filling gaps in information with assumptions. Those assumptions often lead to frustration or mistrust. Over time, these misunderstandings create distance between people who might otherwise work well together.

Communication prevents that distance from forming.

Leaders who communicate effectively provide clarity during uncertainty. Educators who communicate clearly remove confusion that might otherwise discourage students. Teams that communicate openly strengthen trust among their members. Communication also requires vulnerability. Speaking honestly about challenges, uncertainties, and expectations requires courage. Yet that vulnerability is precisely what allows individuals to grow together. Communication sustains unity. But even the clearest communication cannot remove one unavoidable aspect of growth: challenge. At some point, every individual will face moments where progress becomes difficult. Mistakes will occur. Failure will appear. Doubt may begin to creep in. When that happens, communication alone cannot carry someone forward. Something deeper must exist within each individual.

That next brick is confidence.

Because progress requires the belief that growth is still possible.

Chapter 9

Confidence: The Fifth Brick

"Success is not final, failure is not fatal: it is the courage to continue that counts."

Winston Churchill

Confidence

During the early days of World War II, Nazi Germany was rapidly conquering Europe. Many leaders at that time believed that Britain would soon fall as well and succumb to the fate of Hitler's goal of taking over all of Europe. The newly appointed Prime Minister of Britain, Winston Churchill, felt otherwise. In one of his most famous speeches to Parliament, Churchill refused to accept defeat and declared that Britain would "fight on the beaches…fight on the landing grounds….and never surrender." While his speech did not create a magic end to the war, he gave the British people something powerful—confidence that continuing to fight did matter. Churchill's leadership reminds us that confidence is not the absence of fear; it is the decision to keep moving forward despite the fear.

Confidence does not emerge from comfort.

Confidence grows through challenge, through repeated attempts, and often through failure. Individuals who have never struggled may not develop a deep sense of confidence because they have never been forced to overcome adversity.

Failure plays a critical role in developing confidence. In education, students must learn that mistakes are not signs of weakness but essential steps in growth. A classroom that punishes failure creates fear. A classroom that treats failure as a learning opportunity builds resilience. Confidence allows individuals to move forward even when success is uncertain. Students who believe they are capable of improvement approach challenges differently than those who believe ability is fixed. Educators who encourage growth cultivate confidence that extends beyond academic achievement. Confidence is not arrogance. Arrogance dismisses the possibility of failure. Confidence recognizes difficulty but proceeds anyway.

Athletes understand this principle well. Training involves repeated setbacks and adjustments. Each failure provides information that leads to improvement. Education functions in much the same way. Students must attempt difficult tasks, receive feedback, and try again. Over time, this process builds confidence that becomes internal rather than dependent on external validation.

Confidence is the fifth brick because individuals must believe they are capable of moving forward. Confidence breaks down the internal walls that fear builds.

Comfort rarely stretches our abilities or reveals our potential. True confidence grows through repeated exposure to challenge—through moments where success is uncertain, but effort continues anyway. This is why failure plays such an important role in growth. Failure provides information. It reveals weaknesses that can be strengthened and strategies that must be adjusted. Each attempt, even unsuccessful ones, builds resilience. Students who learn to view failure as part of the process become far more capable learners.

Athletes understand this instinctively. Training involves repetition, adjustment, and persistence. Progress rarely happens overnight. Confidence emerges gradually as individuals recognize their ability to overcome obstacles.

Education works in much the same way. When students believe they can improve, they approach challenges differently. They become willing to attempt difficult tasks because they trust their ability to learn through the process.

Healthcare providers who trust their training and preparation are more willing to engage in complex situations, communicate clearly under pressure, and make informed decisions. That confidence is not rooted in certainty, but in experience, and the ability to learn from both success and failure.

Confidence encourages effort. Yet confidence must be directed carefully. When confidence becomes centered only on personal success, it can unintentionally shift focus away from others. True leadership requires more than belief in oneself. It requires a willingness to elevate others.

Confidence must therefore be paired with humility.

That humility leads directly to the next brick—servanthood.

Because leadership reaches its greatest strength when it serves something larger than itself.

Chapter 10

Servanthood: The Sixth Brick

"The greatest among you will be your servant."

Matthew 23:11 (NIV)

Servanthood

In the final week of His life on Earth, Jesus Christ spoke to a large crowd gathered at the Temple of Jerusalem, His disciples among them. It was a moment of preparation and teaching. Not just for what was coming next, but for the kind of leadership they would be called to carry forward.

The message challenged everything they understood about leadership. The religious leaders of the time held authority, status, and recognition. But Jesus made it clear, authority alone does not define leadership. Position does not create influence. Titles do not earn trust.

Instead, Jesus pointed to something different. Leadership is not about being served, it's about serving others. He warned against leaders who seek recognition over responsibility, and status over sacrifice.

Jesus wanted those listening to understand that true leadership and true authority are earned through active participation and sacrifice, rather than just holding a position of high rank and giving commands.

Leadership reaches its highest form when it becomes service.

Servanthood challenges the traditional view of authority. Instead of focusing on how the team serves the leader, it shifts the focus to how the leader serves others. This principle appears in both effective leadership models and spiritual teachings. True influence is not built through dominance, but through humility and a commitment to the well-being of others.

In education, servanthood transforms the role of the educator. Teachers do not exist to elevate their own status or authority. Their purpose is to equip students with the knowledge, skills, and confidence necessary to succeed beyond the classroom.

In business, servanthood reshapes the role of leadership. A leader's purpose is to develop people, remove obstacles, and create environments where others can perform at their highest level. When leaders choose to serve, they build trust that drives performance, not fear that controls it. The strongest organizations are not built on authority alone, but on leaders who invest in their teams, hold them accountable, and elevate them to exceed what they thought was possible.

In healthcare, servanthood brings the focus back to what matters most—the person in front of you. Providers do not exist to simply diagnose, treat, and move on. Their purpose is to care, to listen, and to advocate for patients in moments when they are most vulnerable. True impact is not measured only in outcomes, but in how patients feel seen, heard, and supported throughout their care. When healthcare professionals lead with servanthood, they create trust, improve outcomes, and recognize every patient not as a chart, but as a life of inherent value—one deserving of attention, dignity, and the highest level of care.

Servanthood requires empathy.

Understanding the challenges students face allows educators to meet them where they are. This does not mean lowering expectations; rather, it means providing the guidance and support necessary to reach those expectations. Leaders who serve others create loyalty and respect that cannot be commanded through authority alone. Servanthood dismantles ego-driven leadership. It replaces control with mentorship and replaces distance with connection. Walls often form when individuals feel overlooked or undervalued. Servanthood breaks those walls by placing others at the center of leadership.

The same applies to healthcare professionals. In healthcare, the true measure of effectiveness goes beyond clinical knowledge—it is found in the ability to understand the human experience behind the condition. Patients arrive carrying more than symptoms; they bring fear, uncertainty, and often a loss of control. Addressing this does not weaken the standard of care—it strengthens it. When providers take the time to communicate clearly, listen intentionally, and involve patients in their care, they build trust that no title or credential can demand. Servanthood shifts the focus from simply treating conditions to genuinely care for people. It replaces transactional encounters with meaningful engagement and turns moments of vulnerability into opportunities for connection. When patients feel overlooked, barriers form quickly. But when they feel valued and understood, those barriers begin to fall, creating space for better outcomes and a stronger, more human-centered standard of care.

Leadership driven by ego seeks recognition.

Leadership driven by service creates impact.

Servanthood is the sixth brick because leadership ultimately exists to elevate others.

Servanthood strengthens every relationship within an organization. But for servanthood to truly take root, it must exist within an environment that allows it to flourish. Even the most dedicated servant leader cannot thrive in an environment that discourages growth, connection, and collaboration. Culture matters. The environment determines whether the values of leadership, integrity, unity, communication, confidence, and servanthood will endure.

Which brings us to the final brick.

Environment.

Because culture ultimately determines whether a foundation stands strong.

Chapter 11

Environment: The Seventh Brick

"Culture eats strategy for breakfast."

Peter Drucker

Environment

London – 1934: A young man attends a lecture at Cambridge University. The lecturer was the extremely popular economist John Maynard Keynes, who was widely regarded as one of the most influential economic thinkers in the world at that time. Keynes' ideas were revolutionary during the Great Depression because they argued that governments should actively intervene in the economy to stimulate demand and reduce unemployment—an idea that was reshaping economic policy across Europe and the United States. After the lecture, the students who attended were excitedly discussing Keynes' brilliant economic formulas and theories. One young man later wrote that while listening to him, he realized something important: Keynes had made economics about the behavior of money, but the more important question was about the behavior of people inside institutions. That young man was Peter Drucker. Drucker concluded that the future would depend less on economic theory and more on how organizations were led and how people worked together within them. That realization ultimately led to the ideas that established him as the father of modern management.

Throughout his work, Drucker emphasized that the true driving force behind any successful organization is not simply strategy, policies, or procedures, but the culture that surrounds the people within it. His famous observation that "culture eats strategy for breakfast" reflects the idea that no matter how carefully a plan is designed, it will fail if the environment in which it is implemented does not support it. Leaders must intentionally shape the environments around them, because culture ultimately determines whether individuals merely exist within a system or truly thrive within it.

Environment shapes behavior more than most individuals realize.

The culture surrounding a group influences attitudes, expectations, and outcomes. Individuals respond to the environments in which they are placed.

In education, the classroom environment determines whether students feel motivated or disengaged.

In the corporate environment, organizational culture plays a critical role in shaping whether both employees and leaders feel prepared, supported, and capable of meeting the expectations placed upon them each day.

In healthcare, the clinical environment directly influences whether providers feel equipped and confident in delivering the level of care that patients not only require but expect.

A supportive environment encourages curiosity and persistence. A negative environment suppresses participation and discourages effort. The environment includes more than a physical space. It encompasses attitudes, expectations, relationships, and emotional climate. A classroom may be well-equipped with resources, but if the environment lacks encouragement and respect, those resources will not translate into meaningful learning.

Leaders shape environment through their actions. When leaders demonstrate integrity, communication, and servanthood, those values begin to permeate the culture around them. Over time, the environment reflects the character of the leadership guiding it. Positive environments encourage growth. Negative environments reinforce limitations. Students who believe they are capable of improvement work harder and persist longer. Teams that trust their environment take risks necessary for innovation.

Environment is the seventh brick because culture determines whether the foundation thrives. A strong environment ensures that the other six bricks remain secure. The environment determines the direction in which people grow. The attitudes, expectations, and behaviors that surround individuals shape how they think, how they act, and what they believe is possible. The environment is often the most influential factor in personal and professional development. Settings grounded in encouragement, accountability, and respect foster confidence, resilience, and growth. Within these environments, challenges are no longer viewed as obstacles, but as opportunities to improve, adapt, and move forward.

In contrast, environments built on fear or indifference quickly suppress motivation. The same is true in organizations and teams. Positive environments amplify leadership, integrity, unity, communication, confidence, and servanthood. Negative environments slowly undermine them. The environment acts as the atmosphere surrounding the foundation. If the atmosphere is supportive, growth accelerates. If the atmosphere is hostile or discouraging, even strong foundations begin to weaken. Leaders must therefore become intentional architects of the environment. They must cultivate spaces where individuals feel safe to grow, where collaboration is encouraged, and where effort is recognized.

When the environment is strong, the seven bricks begin reinforcing one another. Leadership provides direction. Integrity builds trust. Unity strengthens collaboration. Communication ensures clarity. Confidence encourages resilience. Servanthood fosters humility. The environment sustains them all. But even a strong foundation requires something more. Bricks alone do not hold themselves together. There must be something that binds them, fills the gaps, absorbs the pressure, and holds everything in place.

Chapter 12

Faith: The Mortar Between the Bricks

"Therefore everyone who hears these words of mine and puts them into practice is like a wise man who built his house on the rock."

Matthew 7:24 (NIV)

Faith: The Mortar Between the Bricks

In chapter 1, I mentioned the concept of both the bricks and the mortar. As we have worked through each of the seven bricks—leadership, integrity, unity, communication, confidence, servanthood, and environment—one thing becomes clear: bricks alone are not enough.

Bricks are designed to be strong. They can be well placed with careful thought and intention. However, they remain separate pieces of the overall structure we are trying to build. The foundation requires these important bricks to be held together, or the resulting outcome doesn't create a lasting impact, it creates another structure ready to crumble and fail. Individually these bricks remain separate pieces. Separate ideas that help to create something powerful but still lacking that one component that ties it all together. This is where the mortar comes in. Mortar is what binds everything together. It fills the gaps, creates stability and ensures that what is being built as a foundation can withstand the pressure, the time, and the adversity.

For me, that mortar is faith. Not as an abstract idea, but as something foundational to how I lead, how I respond, and how I continue forward when things are uncertain. The principles of the seven bricks are not enough without the deeper connection holding it all in place.

Leadership alone is not enough.

Integrity will be tested, and often.

Unity will be strained.

Communication will break down.

Confidence will waver.

Servanthood will feel inconvenient.

Even the strongest environments will face pressure.

When those moments come, there must be something deeper holding it all together. Faith provides that anchor.

It allows me to lead when outcomes are uncertain. It grounds my integrity when compromise would be easier. It preserves unity when division feels easier than understanding. It sustains confidence when results don't come immediately. It strengthens communication when clarity is difficult. It keeps my focus on serving others rather than serving myself. Ultimately, it stabilizes the environment when everything around me feels unsettled.

Faith does not eliminate failure. But it changes how I respond to it. It reminds me that my identity is not defined by setbacks. That my purpose is not limited by my circumstances, and it reinforces that what I am building has meaning beyond what can be immediately seen.

Without mortar, bricks shift and crack. They begin to fall apart under pressure. Without something holding it all together, leadership becomes inconsistent and growth becomes unstable.

My faith in Jesus Christ and His teachings on leadership have shaped how I lead and serve others. It has helped shape not just what I build, but how I impact the people around me. This foundation is not only about personal growth. It is about influence. It is about the impact your life and leadership can have on others.

The foundation becomes complete.

But even strong foundations require ongoing attention. Because walls, if ignored long enough, have a way of returning.

Which leads to the final chapter: Keeping the walls down.

Chapter 13

Keeping the Walls Down

"We are what we repeatedly do. Excellence, then, is not an act but a habit."

Aristotle

Keeping the Walls Down

The ultimate goal is not simply personal success. The goal is influence that extends beyond ourselves. The kind that extends beyond your position, your title, and even your lifetime.

When we teach others how to build strong foundations rather than defensive walls, we contribute to a culture where collaboration replaces isolation and growth replaces fear. Walls may appear strong, but they divide people. Foundations bring people together. And when the right bricks are placed carefully and consistently, those foundations can support generations to come. Breaking down walls is not a one-time event. Walls form gradually through fear, misunderstanding, pride, and failure. Even after they are dismantled, they can begin rebuilding themselves if we stop paying attention to the foundation beneath us.

You don't drift back into strong foundations; you drift back into walls.

That's why the seven bricks are not ideas to understand—they are disciplines to live.

- **Leadership** calls you forward when it would be easier to retreat.
- **Integrity** holds the line when no one is watching.
- **Unity** reminds you that success was never meant to be built alone.
- **Communication** keeps small cracks from becoming major fractures.
- **Confidence** gives you the courage to keep building, even after failure.
- **Servanthood** keeps your focus where it belongs—on lifting others.
- **Environment** protects what you've built from slowly eroding over time.

Individually, each brick matters. Together, they are unshakeable.

Because together, they don't just replace walls—they create something far stronger. They create a foundation. And foundations change everything. Foundations allow growth instead of guarding against it. They create connection instead of separation. They give people something solid to stand on—so they can become more than they ever could alone.

Every student who learns to build with these bricks carries them forward—into their families, their careers, and their communities. Every educator who models these principles doesn't just teach lessons—they shape lives. Every leader, whether in a classroom, a boardroom, or a locker room—sets the tone for what gets built. In business, foundations determine whether teams collaborate or compete against each other in ways that erode trust. They determine whether people feel valued or simply managed. The strongest organizations aren't held together by pressure or control, they're built on clarity, trust, and shared purpose.

In the world of athletics, the same truth shows up even faster. Talent alone doesn't sustain success. Teams built on ego fracture under pressure, but teams built on trust, communication, and accountability find a way to endure. When the foundation is right, individuals don't just play for themselves, they play for something greater.

I've seen this close up as an athletic trainer. Injuries don't just test the body; they reveal the foundation beneath the team. In those moments, you find out quickly who shows up, who communicates, who leads, and who pulls away. The teams that are built on strong foundations don't splinter when adversity hits, they tighten. They support. They respond with purpose instead of panic. And in leadership at any level, the pattern is the same. People often don't rise to the level of what is demanded. They rise to the level of what is consistently built around them.

This is how impact multiplies. This is how influence outlives you.

At the beginning, the walls didn't feel like walls. They felt like protection. They felt necessary. They were built in response to pressure, disappointment, fear, and moments that left a mark. Brick by brick, they went up quickly, often without intention, until what once felt like safety slowly became separation.

That's where this journey began.

But somewhere along the way, something shifted. What once felt like strength was revealed to be limitation. What once kept you safe was also keeping others at a distance. And in that realization, a new choice emerged; not just to tear those walls down, but to become intentional about what would replace them.

The goal was never just to tear down walls. The goal is to build something stronger in their place.

Pause for a moment and take inventory. What have you been building without realizing it? What habits, responses, and patterns have quietly become your structure? Because whether you intended to or not, something is being built every day.

The question is not if you are building—it's whether what you are building is worth standing on.

When the seven bricks work together, the foundation becomes capable of supporting extraordinary growth. When individuals learn to build foundations rather than walls, they create environments where others can thrive long after they are gone. But even the strongest foundation depends on what holds it together. Without the right mortar, even well-placed bricks will begin to shift. Time will reveal the weaknesses. This is where faith matters. It is what holds everything in place when uncertainty arises.

You don't get to go back now.

You don't get to build carelessly.

You don't get to ignore the cracks forming beneath you.

You don't get to lead halfway.

You've been given the blueprint now.

The final question that remains is:

What will you build with it?

Because the people around you—whether you realize it or not—are already building on what you create. Walls divide people. But foundations bring them together. And what you build today will determine what stands long after you're gone.

In the end, you won't be remembered for the walls you hid behind—only for what you built that others could stand on.

www.ingramcontent.com/pod-product-compliance
Lightning Source LLC
LaVergne TN
LVHW010627100826
845148LV00014B/3151

* 9 7 9 8 2 3 4 0 4 2 6 1 3 *